The

WOOD WORKER'S POCKET PALETTE

Instant, practical, visual guidance on mixing and matching stains and other wood finishes

Nigel Lofthouse

B.T. Batsford Ltd • London

A QUARTO BOOK
First published in
Great Britain by
B. T. Batsford Ltd.
4 Fitzhardinge Street
London W1H 0AH

ISBN 0-7134-7231-6

A catalogue record
for this book is
available from the
British Library.

This book was
designed and
produced by Quarto
Publishing plc
The Old Brewery
6 Blundell Street
London N7 9BH

While every care
has been taken with
the printing of the
colour charts, the
publishers cannot
guarantee total
accuracy in every case.

Red oak
page 10

White oak
page 14

Rock maple
page 30

American walnut
page 34

White ash
page 48

Ponderosa pine
page 52

English oak
page **20**

American whitewood
page **26**

English walnut
page **38**

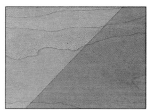

American cherry
page **44**

White pine
page **56**

Cedar of Lebanon
page **60**

CONTENTS

USING THIS BOOK

THE PURPOSE OF THIS BOOK is to provide the woodworker with an easy guide to different wood finishes. The reasons for finishing wood are to change its colour or texture and to protect the surface from dirt, heat and spilt liquids. This can be achieved with very many methods which give varying degrees of protection. In simple terms the more time you spend working up a surface, the better protection you will provide.

Choice of timbers
Twelve of the most commer-cially available woods are featured in this book – you will find hardwoods on pages 10-51, softwoods on pages 52-63.

Symbols
At-a-glance symbols sum-marize the most important characteristics of each wood. For an explanation of symbols see page 9.

Manufactured stains
These are commercial stains, ranging from the lightest to the darkest to give you a feel for the possibilities. Generic names not trade names have been used to describe the colours they represent.

Always apply a thinned coat of stain first; you can always increase the density but never reduce it without removing the surface of the wood.

Throughout the book, the same stains are shown applied to the twelve different timbers.

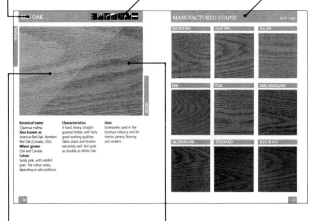

Natural
Planed timber sample in its untreated state, as you would buy it from a timber yard.

Sealed
The timber sample sealed twice and lightly sanded between coats; after sealing two coats of wax polish have been applied, and the surface burnished to a shine.

Preparing the surface and final finishing for manufactured stains
Each sample has been prepared in the same way (see page 6) and each given the same final finish after staining (see page 8).

In this book we look at 12 different timbers, on each of which we show the effects of nine different manufactured stains; the same 12 timbers are treated to four further treatments based on coloured dyes and erosion techniques; then we show how the woods react to treatments specially tailored for each of them – these special treatments are more complex and should be attempted only when a good degree of confidence has been achieved.

Get fit before you begin: fast repeat arm and hand exercises are essential! You may be rubbing and polishing well into the early hours.

Further treatments
The same further treatments are shown applied to the 12 different timbers.

Special treatments
Finishing treatments tailored to each of the 12 woods.

Coloured dyes
Simple contemporary finishes can be put to exceptional use on new furniture and domestic fittings by combining colours. Coloured dyes are simple to mix or use on mouldings as contrasting details.

Bleached
See page 7 for more information.

Recipes
Step-by-step recipes for you to follow to create the different effects.

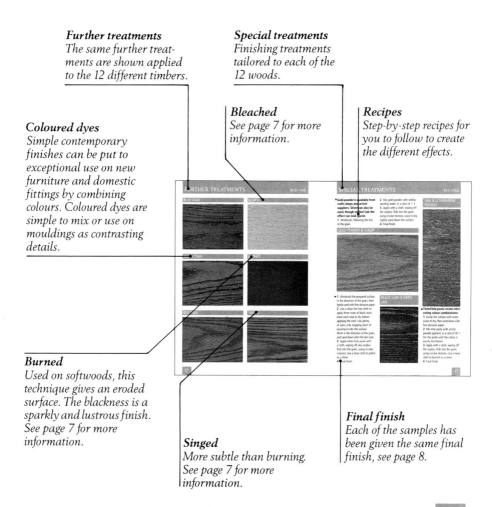

Burned
Used on softwoods, this technique gives an eroded surface. The blackness is a sparkly and lustrous finish. See page 7 for more information.

Singed
More subtle than burning. See page 7 for more information.

Final finish
Each of the samples has been given the same final finish, see page 8.

Timber can be purchased from your supplier in two basic forms – sawn or prepared. Sawn, as its name implies, is simply as it comes off the sawmill, and it is therefore very rough and must be planed to give a surface from which to begin. Only buy sawn timber if you have planing equipment to handle the size you wish to work on.

Prepared timber has been planed industrially and ought to be perfectly flat and square. Check this when you are buying.

Selection of the most suitable piece of wood for the job is important. Choose the best graining for the most visible part of your work, avoiding the softer sapwood for quality or structural parts. Check carefully for knots or faults that you may have missed at the suppliers.

Preparing the surface
Follow the procedure outlined below before tackling any of the effects featured in this book.

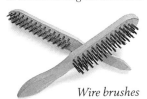

Wire wool

Most of us use mechanical sanding equipment of varying types, orbital hand sanders being the most common. You will need plenty of grades of abrasive paper; buy the best, it saves your arm. Select a grade of paper to remove the wood surface without excessive scratching, then progress through three or four grades to your smoothest paper.

Clean down the timber with a soft brush or clean rag and check the surface in good light for scratches or blemishes. If you are employing a technique which requires burning, singeing or wirebrushing the timber is

Wire brushes

ready to work now. However, other types of finish require that the surface be absolutely smooth. To ensure this, use 0000 grade wire wool, a cabinet scraper or flour paper by hand to give you a perfect surface.

Stripping an existing finish
If you are removing an existing finish consider if you wish to save the original

patina, especially on older furniture. It is very easy to spoil a piece by stripping it back to bare wood. You may be able to clean the existing piece by using 50% turpentine and 50% linseed oil rubbed in until dry, then washed off with slightly soapy warm water. This will remove dirt and old wax finishes to the original finish beneath, leaving you free to re-polish over the original colour.

There are two basic ways of stripping right back to bare wood. A hot-air stripping gun effectively melts the surface, which can then be gently scraped off with a cabinet scraper or wire wool. Chemical paint strippers soften the finish ready to be scraped off. The chemicals used in paint strippers are dangerous; always follow the instructions for safe use.

Silicone-carbide papers and garnet papers for sanding

Applying stains

When applying water-based stain, lightly dampen the surface prior to the first application to increase surface penetration. Use the recommended thinning agent to reduce the

Walnut stain

strength of the stain. Always reduce the stain's strength until you are sure of the depth of colour required, as you cannot easily remove stain without re-preparing your work.

Once you are confident of your colour you can start on your piece. Use a clean rag to wipe the stain along the grain of the timber; try not to overlap strokes, as this will intensify the application. Completely cover the piece, working fairly quickly, then with a dryer part of the same cloth wipe off any excess, again moving with the grain. Leave to dry.

When finishing new wood always cut test pieces of prepared timber to check the strength of colour before you start on your final piece.

TOOLS AND EQUIPMENT

● A wire brush is useful for opening up the grain when applying a limed finish, and for stripping mouldings and carvings.

● Synthetic-bristle brushes can be used to apply bleach.

● A cloth holds more stain than a brush. Keep a supply of clean, lint-free pure cotton cloths for finishing.

● Brushes are best for applying stain to mouldings, corners and carvings.

● Hessian is useful for applying liming paste and other finishes which fill the grain.

● Stockinet (a stretchy machine-knitted cloth) can be used for burnishing to bring a piece up to a final shine.

● Tack rags are useful for wiping dust from shiny surfaces.

Tack rag

Emulsion thinned with water

Burning

Take care when using this technique and always follow the standard safety procedures for using a blowtorch.

For the examples demonstrated in this book, a blowtorch was used to burn the surface almost to charring, then the surface was removed with a wire brush. Don't use this technique on thin boards as they tend to warp very badly.

Singeing

The same rules apply as for burning but the blowtorch is played over the surface gently.

Bleaching

This is a fairly simple technique to use. Most bleaches are supplied in a two-part pack. Always follow the manufacturer's instructions for use. Coloured dyes can be applied onto the bleached timber, giving clear colour on naturally pale timbers.

Thinned emulsion

Thinned down emulsion paint can easily be used to tint pale timber such as American whitewood.

*Metallic powders –
copper, gold
and silver*

Graphite powder
Graphite can be bought in a powder form from hardware shops. It lends wood a soft grey sheen.

Zinc chloride and iron filings
A random and unusual technique, most suited to pale timbers.

Zinc chloride
Zinc chloride on its own, without iron filings, causes timber to take on a dark rich sheen.

Fabric dye
The range of fabric dyes is extensive; when used on pale timbers they can give intense colours.

Liming
Liming is a traditional finish for oak, serving to enhance the appearance of the grain. However, liming can be used on any wood with an open grain. The paste can be tinted with pigment to give interesting light colours, or the timber can be stained before applying the paste.

Metallic powders
Similar to liming, metallic fillers can be used to fill the grain. Mix these powders with sealer before applying.

Branding
Historically, branding used to be called poker work and was an art form in itself. The author has illustrated a very simplified form; you could develop a method to suit yourself.

Final finish
All the examples in this book have been given the same *final* finish.

Apply two coats of sealant (white French polish was used for the examples in this book) and lightly sand the surface between coats. When the sealant is dry, apply a polish (the author used beeswax). Apply sparingly with a clean rag kept solely for the purpose. Always allow early coats of beeswax to dry well, probably overnight. Polish with a clean rag, again kept only for this job. More and more coats can be applied in the same way giving a strong shine. Too much polish applied in one coat will make the surface smeary and difficult to polish. If this occurs wipe the polish off with a turpentine soaked rag and re-polish – as my old grandfather used to say, "more haste, less speed"; I didn't believe him then but I do now!

Graphite powder

Stockinet cloth for burnishing

HEALTH AND SAFETY

Some finishing chemicals are poisonous, flammable or corrosive. Always take care when handling and storing them.

● *Wear protective overalls and gloves.*

● *Wear a mask to protect against dust when sanding and toxic fumes when finishing.*

● *Never store finishes in old food containers or anything that resembles one.*

● *Always keep finishing chemicals well out of reach of children.*

● *Always follow the manufacturer's instructions.*

● *Being environmentally considerate is vitally important. Care and attention must be paid to the disposal of toxic or hazardous chemicals, several of which are used in the treatment of timber. Read the manufacturer's instructions and, if in any doubt, find out from the appropriate authority where and how it is permissible to dispose of them.*

HOW TO USE THE SYMBOLS

Symbols summarize the most important characteristics of each wood. Where appropriate, symbols are graded on a scale of 1 to 5:

1 = poor   4 = very good
2 = fair   5 = excellent
3 = good

 Pre-drilling required
For timbers that require pre-drilling, a pilot hole must be drilled to avoid the wood splitting. If the symbol is absent then the wood does not need to be pre-drilled.

 Ease of working
This symbol indicates the ease of difficulty of cutting or machining wood.

 Suitability for nailing
This gives an indication of whether or not the wood can be successfully nailed without splitting.

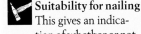 **Suitability for outdoor use**
Woods which rate highly on the scale have a good resistance to sun and weathering.

 Resistance to insect/ fungal attack
This symbol indicates natural resistance to this form of attack.

 Relative weight
This is an important consideration when making items intended to be portable.
For this symbol:
1 = light
2 = medium
3 = fairly heavy
4 = heavy

 Hardwood.

Softwood.

NATURAL

SEALED

Botanical name
Quercus rubra.
Also known as
American Red Oak; Northern Red Oak (Canada, USA).
Where grown
USA and Canada.
Colour
Sandy pink, with reddish grain. The colour varies, depending on soil conditions.

Characteristics
A hard, heavy, straight-grained timber, with fairly good working qualities. Takes stains and finishes extremely well. Not quite as durable as White Oak.

Uses
Extensively used in the furniture industry and for interior joinery, flooring and veneers.

GOLDEN OAK

LIGHT OAK

YELLOW

YEW

TEAK

DARK MAHOGANY

JACOBEAN OAK

ROSEWOOD

BLUE-BLACK

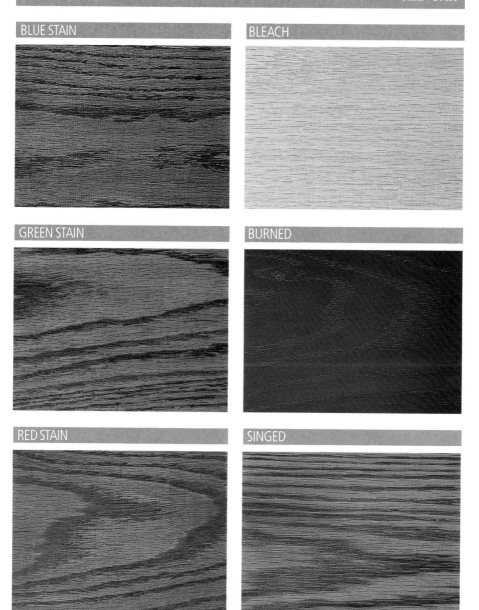

BLUE STAIN

BLEACH

GREEN STAIN

BURNED

RED STAIN

SINGED

▼**Gold powder is available from crafts shops and artists' suppliers. Silver can also be used, though on Red Oak the effect can look garish.**

1 Wirebrush, following the line of the grain.

2 Mix gold powder with shellac sanding sealer, in a ratio of 7:3.
3 Apply with a cloth, wiping off the surplus. Rub into the grain, using circular motions. Leave to dry. Lightly sand down the surface.
4 Final finish.

GOLD POWDER & SEALER

▶**1** Wirebrush the prepared surface in the direction of the grain, then lightly sand with fine abrasive paper.
2 Use a clean lint-free cloth to apply three coats of black stain; leave each coat to dry before applying the next. Use plenty of stain, only stopping short of pouring it onto the surface. Work in the direction of the grain, and sand down after the last coat.
3 Apply white lime paste with a cloth, wiping off any surplus. Rub into the grain, using circular motions. Use a clean cloth to polish to a shine.
4 Final finish.

BLACK STAIN & WHITE LIME

LIME & ULTRAMARINE PIGMENT

▲**Tinted lime paste creates interesting colour combinations.**

1 Damp the surface with water. Leave to dry, then sand down with fine abrasive paper.
2 Mix lime paste with artists' powder pigment, in a ratio of 30:1. Stir the paste until the colour is evenly distributed.
3 Apply with a cloth, wiping off the surplus. Rub into the grain, using circular motions. Use a clean cloth to burnish to a shine.
4 Final finish.

NATURAL

SEALED

Botanical name
Quercus alba.
Also known as
American White Oak and by US regional names.
Where grown
USA and Canada.
Colour
Generally a pale straw colour, with a mid-brown grain fleck. The colour varies considerably from tree to tree.

Characteristics
A hard, heavy oak, with good straight grain. The timber generally works well, though ease of use varies from tree to tree. When quarter-sawn, it displays a silvery grain (similar to English Oak). It stains and finishes very well.

Uses
Furniture, high-quality cabinetwork, flooring, building construction, coffins and boatbuilding. Also used for barrels, as the heartwood is impervious to water.

GOLDEN OAK

LIGHT OAK

YELLOW

YEW

TEAK

DARK MAHOGANY

JACOBEAN OAK

ROSEWOOD

BLUE-BLACK

BLUE STAIN

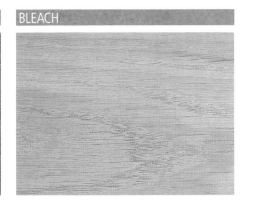

BLEACH

GREEN STAIN

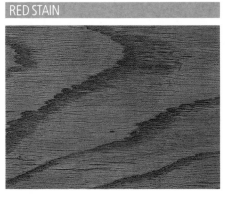

BURNED

RED STAIN

SINGED

►In this example, using tinted lime paste causes the natural darkness of the grain to be reversed, creating a lighter grain and darker background.

1 Damp the surface with water. Leave to dry, then sand down.

2 Mix lime paste with artists' powder pigment, in a ratio of 30:1. Stir the paste until the colour is evenly distributed.

3 Apply the paste with a cloth, wiping off the surplus. Rub into the grain, using circular motions. Burnish with a clean cloth.

4 Final finish.

LIME & GREEN PIGMENT

▼ Gold powder is available from crafts shops and artists' suppliers.

1 Wirebrush, following the line of the grain.

2 Mix gold powder with shellac sanding sealer, in a ratio of 7:3.

3 Apply with a cloth, wiping off the surplus. Rub into the grain, using circular motions. Leave to dry. Sand down.

4 Final finish.

GOLD POWDER & SEALER

BLACK STAIN & WHITE LIME

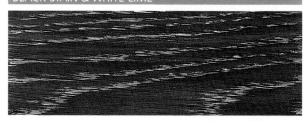

▲1 Wirebrush the surface in the direction of the grain, then lightly sand down.

2 Use a clean lint-free cloth to apply three coats of black stain; leave each coat to dry before applying the next. Use plenty of stain. Work in the direction of the grain, and sand down after the last coat.

3 Apply white lime paste with a cloth, wiping off any surplus. Rub into the grain, using circular motions. Leave to dry.

4 Final finish.

WIREBRUSHING & THINNED EMULSION

◄Peach emulsion is used here and elsewhere because it is a modest colour, in keeping with many wood tones.

1 Wirebrush in the direction of the grain, then sand down lightly.

2 Thin emulsion paint with water, in a ratio of 50:50.

3 Use a clean lint-free cloth to apply the paint, then wipe off any surplus.

4 Rub the paint into the grain, using circular motions. Leave to dry. Lightly sand the surface.

5 Final finish.

Bleached And Dyed

Hall Table and Chair

LEADING FURNITURE DESIGNER John Makepeace uses stains to enhance timbers which are visually dull in their natural state. Washing and bleaching is another technique which he favours to alter the natural colour of some woods. For example, the knot chair shown opposite has been scrubbed several times with caustic soda and a natural bristle brush or wire brush. The brush opens up the grain allowing the caustic soda to bite into the wood, lightening it and lending it a grey, aged appearance.

Constructed of hickory and inspired by the Orient, this desk has been stained in three different colours to enhance what is considered to be a visually dull wood.

English oak and burr elm have been used for this knot chair. The wood has been bleached several times with caustic soda to create a natural-looking aged effect. The designer has deliberately chosen burr with holes, knots and other "imperfections" (see detail).

SEALED

Botanical name
Quercus robur.

Also known as
Pedunculate Oak; French, Polish Oak, etc., according to country of origin.

Where grown
Europe (including UK), Asia Minor and North Africa.

Colour
Generally a pale sandy brown with mid-brown grain fleck, similar to White Oak. Heartwood is darker than sapwood.

Characteristics
An extremely hard, strong, durable timber (the hardness increases with age). The grain is generally straight, but can be quirky. When quarter-sawn, English Oak has a spectacular silver grain. Stains and clear finishes give excellent results. The burr (burl) wood, produced by abnormal growths, is particularly decorative. Acids present in oak corrode ferrous-metal fittings.

Uses
Cabinetwork, furniture, panelling, boatbuilding, church fittings and coffins. Whisky casks are often made from oak, because of the tannic acid in the timber.

GOLDEN OAK

LIGHT OAK

YELLOW

YEW

TEAK

DARK MAHOGANY

JACOBEAN OAK

ROSEWOOD

BLUE-BLACK

BLUE STAIN

BLEACH

GREEN STAIN

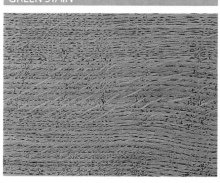

BURNED

RED STAIN

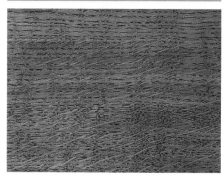

SINGED

WIREBRUSHING & THINNED EMULSION

▲ **The emulsion is thinned to lighten the colour, give better penetration, and allow you to more easily wipe off any surplus paint. Any colour emulsion can be used to suit the job.**

1 Wirebrush in the direction of the grain, then sand lightly.
2 Thin emulsion paint with water, in a ratio of 50:50.
3 Use a clean lint-free cloth to apply the paint, then wipe off any surplus.
4 Rub the paint into the grain, using circular motions. Leave to dry, then sand.
5 Final finish.

▼**1** Damp the surface with water. Leave to dry, then sand down with fine abrasive paper.
2 Use a clean lint-free cloth to apply green stain. Use plenty of stain, only stopping short of pouring it onto the surface. Work in the direction of the grain.

STAIN & TINTED LIME PASTE

Lightly sand down.
3 Mix lime paste with artists' powder pigment, in a ratio of 30:1.
4 Apply the paste with a cloth, wiping off the surplus. Rub into the grain, using circular motions. Use a clean cloth to burnish to a shine.
5 Final finish.

GOLD POWDER & SEALER

◄**The fairly tight grain in this example resulted in less gold powder being taken up. The result is less dramatic than other more open-grained examples.**

1 Wirebrush, following the line of the grain.
2 Mix gold powder with shellac sanding sealer, in a ratio of 7:3. Stir in the gold powder until it is evenly distributed throughout the sealer.
3 Apply with a cloth, wiping off the surplus. Rub into the grain, using circular motions. Use a clean cloth to burnish to a shine.
4 Final finish.

ENGLISH OAK DYED AND LIMED

Pedestal Table

THE DRAMATIC USE of a traditional finish combined with natural oak and leather inlays create weight and power in this pedestal table by Nigel Lofthouse. The strongly grained wood has been specially selected for dyeing and liming for the top of the piece, and for dyeing only for the central boss.

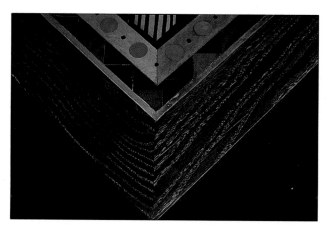

▲ *A detail of the table top clearly shows where the wood has been dyed black and limed.*

▶ *The base of the pedestal shows natural oak built up in large staggered sections and turned on a lathe. After sanding down, the four beaded sections were carefully dyed while the machine was running. The bosses were dyed and applied later.*

An unusual use of dyed leather inlay is bordered by black limed oak to give a strong intricate effect. Dyeing and liming can also be used to good effect on large areas, table tops and fitted furniture.

NATURAL

SEALED

Botanical name

Liriodendron tulipifera.

Also known as

Poplar (incorrectly), Canary Wood, Canary Whitewood, Tulip Tree, Tulip Wood; Yellow Poplar, Hickory Poplar, Popple, Saddle Tree (USA).

Where grown

USA and Canada.

Colour

Light cream, streaked with grey and pale brown.

Characteristics

A comparatively light timber that has a very smooth texture. It is easy to work, and takes stains and finishes well if applied with care. However, it is not particularly strong or durable and is prone to fungal attack. Do not confuse this hardwood with the common softwood known as whitewood. The burr (burl) wood is sometimes called "Green Cyprus Burr".

Uses

Interior doors, joinery and cabinetwork. Extensively used for woodcarving and sculpture and in making plywood.

GOLDEN OAK

LIGHT OAK

YELLOW

YEW

TEAK

DARK MAHOGANY

JACOBEAN OAK

ROSEWOOD

BLUE-BLACK

BLUE STAIN

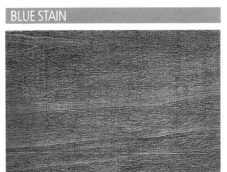

BLEACH

GREEN STAIN

BURNED

RED STAIN

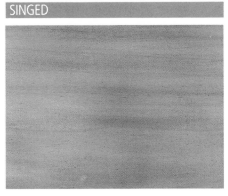

SINGED

► Graphite powder is available from hardware stores. It imparts a grey sheen to the surface of wood.

1 Dip a clean lint-free cloth into powdered graphite, and rub in with the grain.

2 Use a clean cloth to burnish to a shine.

3 Final finish.

GRAPHITE POWDER

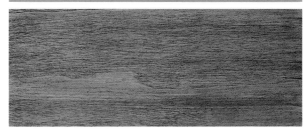

IRON FILINGS & ZINC CHLORIDE

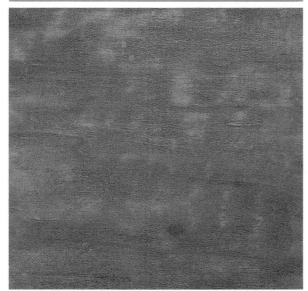

▼ American Whitewood is a relatively grain-free timber. When tinting with emulsion, you get an all-over colour.

1 Damp the surface with water. Leave to dry, then sand down with fine abrasive paper.

2 Dilute emulsion with water, in a ratio of 50:50.

3 Use a clean lint-free cloth to apply the paint. Wipe off any surplus.

4 Rub the paint into the grain, using circular motions. Leave to dry, then lightly sand.

5 Final finish.

THINNED EMULSION

▲ Any expert in timber treatments would be hard pushed to guess how this effect was achieved, but for a bland timber such as American Whitewood it provides an interesting texture and colour combination.

1 Pour zinc chloride onto the wood, enough to cover the surface. Dab it around with a clean lint-free cloth.

2 Randomly scatter iron filings onto the surface. Leave for 24 hours.

3 Wash off with copious amounts of water. Leave to dry, then sand down.

4 Final finish.

NATURAL

SEALED

Botanical name
Acer saccharum.
Also known as
Hard Maple, Sugar Maple; White Maple (USA).
Where grown
Canada and USA.
Colour
Very pale, with a pinkish tinge and pinky grey grain. The heartwood is purple brown (similar to walnut).

Characteristics
A very hard, strong, even-textured timber, with good bending properties.
The attractive grain sometimes has a curving or wavy pattern. Since it is difficult to work, a reduced cutting angle is often necessary, especially on curvy or wavy grain. To avoid uneven staining, you may need to preseal the surface with French polish, then layer the stain between coats.

Uses
Because it is smooth and hard-wearing, Rock Maple is used for flooring and butcher's blocks. It is also an excellent timber for furniture and turning. Maple veneers with a distinctive bird's-eye pattern are highly prized.

GOLDEN OAK

LIGHT OAK

YELLOW

YEW

TEAK

DARK MAHOGANY

JACOBEAN OAK

ROSEWOOD

BLUE-BLACK

BLUE STAIN

BLEACH

GREEN STAIN

BURNED & SANDED

RED STAIN

SINGED

▼ **Rock Maple is a tricky wood to stain without the result looking patchy. Because of its variable absorbency, take great care to sand down thoroughly before applying the dye.**

1 Apply undiluted liquid fabric dye, using a clean lint-free cloth.

Stain the piece thoroughly, then wipe off any surplus dye.

2 Rub into the grain, using circular motions. Leave to dry.

3 Apply more coats, depending on the depth of colour you want to achieve. Sand down after applying the last coat.

4 Final finish.

GREEN FABRIC DYE

RED FABRIC DYE

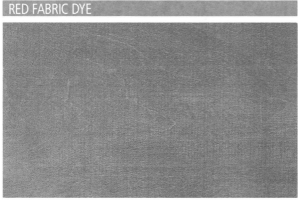

▲ **Bright colours can look very effective on this pale wood. Three coats of fabric dye were used on this sample.**

1 Apply undiluted liquid fabric dye, using a clean lint-free cloth. Stain the piece thoroughly, then wipe off any surplus.

2 Rub into the grain, using circular motions. Leave to dry, then sand down. Apply more coats, depending on the depth of colour required.

3 Final finish.

▶ **The rhubarb imparts a very pale colour change. Rhubarb leaves are toxic when eaten; don't store the mulch in food containers, and throw away the pulp after use.**

1 Process rhubarb leaves in a food blender, reducing them to a pulp. Wash and dry the blender thoroughly after use.

2 Lay the pulp thickly on the surface of the timber and leave for 24 hours.

3 Wash off with copious amounts of water. Leave to dry, then sand down.

4 Final finish.

RHUBARB LEAVES

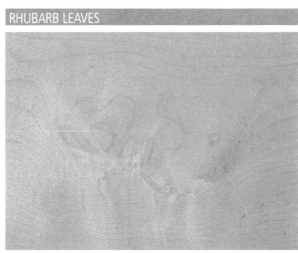

NATURAL

SEALED

Botanical name

Juglans nigra.

Also known as

Canaletto, Black Hickory Nut, Canadian Walnut, Walnut Tree; Black American Walnut, Virginia Walnut (UK); Black Walnut (UK, USA).

Where grown

USA and Canada.

Colour

An unusual purplish grey and mid-brown, with evenly flecked grain.

Characteristics

American Walnut is mostly straight-grained, with occasional wavy figuring. A very hard and durable timber, it works cleanly and has exceptionally good bending qualities. The wood shrinks very little in use. Burr (burl), butt and curl walnut veneers are particularly attractive; butt veneers are cut from the stump of the tree, curl veneers from the fork of the trunk.

Uses

High-quality cabinetwork and furniture, turning and carving, gun stocks, clock cases and musical instruments.

GOLDEN OAK

LIGHT OAK

YELLOW

YEW

TEAK

DARK MAHOGANY

JACOBEAN OAK

ROSEWOOD

BLUE-BLACK

BLUE STAIN

BLEACH

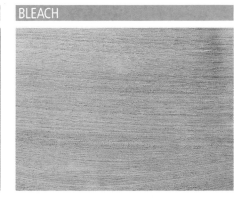

GREEN STAIN

BURNED & WIREBRUSHED

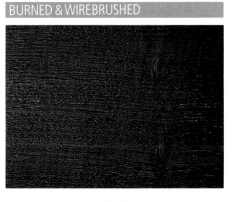

RED STAIN

SINGED

Compare the sample below with the one on the right. The wire brush has opened the grain, resulting in more lime penetrating the surface.

WIREBRUSHING & WHITE LIME

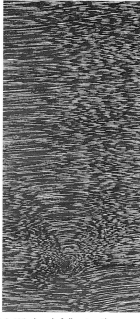

▲**1** Wirebrush following the direction of the grain.

2 Use a clean lint-free cloth to apply lime paste, taking care to cover the surface. Wipe off any surplus.

3 Rub into the grain, using circular motions. Try to keep the pressure even. Use a clean cloth to burnish to a shine.

4 Final finish.

WHITE LIME

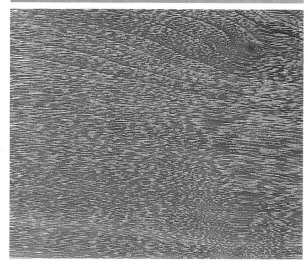

▲**1** Damp the surface with water. Leave the wood to dry, then sand down lightly, using fine abrasive paper.

2 Use a clean lint-free cloth to apply the lime paste, taking care to cover the surface. Wipe off any surplus.

3 Rub into the grain, using circular motions. Use a clean cloth to burnish to a shine.

4 Final finish.

IRON FILINGS & ZINC CHLORIDE

◄**This naturally dark timber can be darkened even further by the application of iron filings and zinc chloride. The result is a rich, dense effect.**

1 Pour on enough zinc chloride to cover the surface, and dab it around with a clean lint-free cloth.

2 Randomly scatter iron filings onto the surface. Leave for 24 hours.

3 Wash off with copious amounts of water. Leave to dry, then sand down.

4 Final finish.

NATURAL

SEALED

Botanical name
Juglans regia.
Also known as
French, Italian, Turkish Walnut, etc., according to country of origin.
Where grown
Europe, Asia Minor and south west Asia.
Colour
A rich, chocolate brown, with darker cross grain.

Characteristics
English Walnut has a predominantly straight grain, with wavy figuring that has an attractive sheen. A delightfully characterful wood, it is good to work, polishes well, and is highly shock-resistant. However, the effects of staining are limited due to its dark natural colour.

Uses
High-quality furniture and veneers, gun stocks, turning and carving, marquetry and panelling.

GOLDEN OAK

LIGHT OAK

YELLOW

YEW

TEAK

DARK MAHOGANY

JACOBEAN OAK

ROSEWOOD

BLUE-BLACK

BLUE STAIN

BLEACH

GREEN STAIN

BURNED

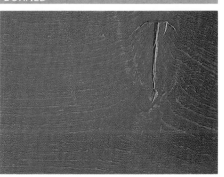

RED STAIN

SINGED

▼ **Walnut is a hard wood and therefore needs quite severe wirebrushing to open up the grain.**

1 Wirebrush following the direction of the grain.

2 Use a clean lint-free cloth to apply lime paste, taking care to cover the surface. Wipe off any surplus lime paste.

3 Rub into the grain, using circular motions. Use a clean cloth to burnish to a shine.

4 Final finish.

WIREBRUSHING & WHITE LIME

IRON FILINGS & ZINC CHLORIDE

▲ **Zinc chloride darkens walnut to a nearly black finish; the iron filings leave a lighter area with a pinky orange tinge.**

1 Pour on enough zinc chloride to cover the surface, and dab it around with a clean lint-free cloth.

2 Randomly scatter iron filings onto the surface. Leave for 24 hours.

3 Wash off with copious amounts of water. Leave to dry, then lightly sand down.

4 Final finish.

▶ **Use only as much oil as it takes to ease the graphite over the surface – too much will flood the surface and the wood will not dry out.**

1 Dip a clean lint-free cloth into powdered graphite and rub in with the grain.

2 Use another cloth to apply oil to the surface. Take care not to apply too much oil to the wood. Rub in, using circular motions. Leave the wood to dry thoroughly before going on to the next step.

3 Final finish.

OIL & GRAPHITE

INLAID STAINED VENEERS

Boxes

INLAYING DYED VENEERS gives a bold architectural feeling to these pieces by Nicholas Pryke. Pure silver inlay has then been added to this intricate pattern. The designer has used commercially produced veneers, which are available with coloured or natural finishes. All Pryke's pieces are meticulously constructed and extremely detailed in their graphic imagery.

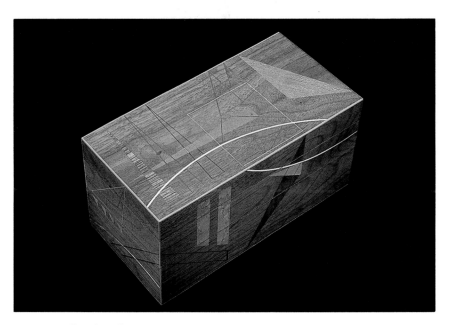

A jewellery box showing a very fine use of English walnut with natural inlaid timber and dyed veneers. The pure silver inlay gives a rich quality to the work.

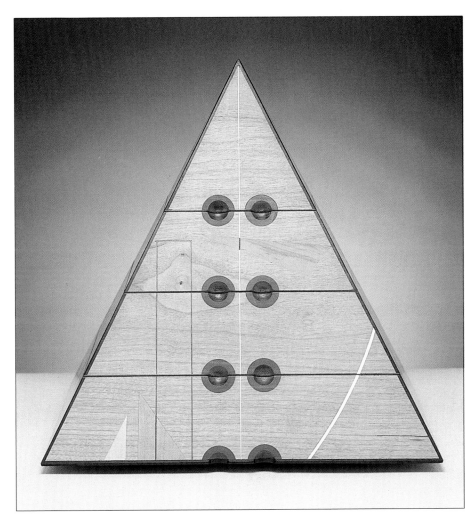

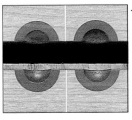

◄ *A detail of the pyramid box (shown above) showing the darker coloured drawer-pulls.*

▲ *Although the construction of this box is complex, the clever use of small areas of inlaid colour is a strong factor in the design, as are the black edge bandings which emphasize the geometric design.*

NATURAL

SEALED

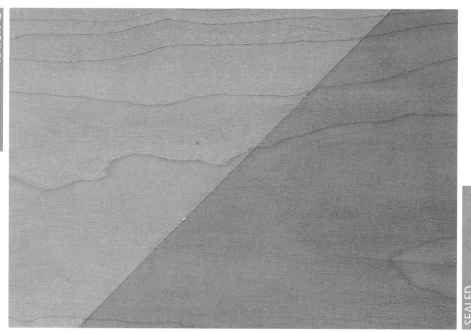

Botanical name
Prunus serotina.
Also known as
Wild Cherry, Whiskey Cherry; Black Cherry (Canada, USA); Cabinet Cherry (USA).
Where grown
Amongst deciduous forests in Canada and USA.
Colour
Has an attractive pinkish tinge, with darker grain. The heartwood is a deeper red or reddish brown. Gum pockets are dark brown.

Characteristics
A fine, smooth-grained timber of medium strength. The grain is straight, with occasional attractive figuring and small gum pockets. Cherry is easy to work, bends well, and is an excellent wood for turning. It stains and polishes well.

Uses
High-class joinery and interior fittings, furniture, pattern making, turning, and musical instruments.

GOLDEN OAK

LIGHT OAK

YELLOW

YEW

TEAK

DARK MAHOGANY

JACOBEAN OAK

ROSEWOOD

BLUE-BLACK

BLUE STAIN

BLEACH

GREEN STAIN

BURNED & SANDED

RED STAIN

SINGED

▼1 Damp the surface with water. Leave to dry, then sand down.

2 Thin the emulsion paint with water, in a ratio of 50:50.

3 Apply the paint, then wipe off any surplus.

4 Rub the paint into the grain, using circular motions. Leave to dry, then lightly sand.

5 Final finish.

ZINC CHLORIDE

THINNED EMULSION

▲American Cherry can be made to resemble walnut by applying zinc chloride. The longer you leave the zinc chloride, the more definite the blackish brown colour will be.

1 Damp the surface with water. Leave to dry, then sand down with fine abrasive paper.

2 Pour on enough zinc chloride to cover the surface. Using a dabbing action, move the zinc chloride around with a clean lint-free cloth.

3 Wash off with copious amounts of water. Leave to dry, then sand down.

4 Final finish.

▶When dry, writing ink leaves a beautiful metallic sheen on the wood's surface. The blue colour imparted by ink is rich and dense.

1 Apply undiluted ink, using a clean lint-free cloth. Stain the piece thoroughly, then wipe off any surplus.

2 Rub into the grain, using circular motions. Leave to dry then sand down. Apply more coats, depending on the depth of the colour required.

3 Final finish.

INK

NATURAL

SEALED

Botanical name
Fraxinus americana.

Also known as
American Ash, American White Ash; Canadian Ash (UK).

Where grown
USA and Canada.

Colour
Fairly yellow, with a pronounced darker grain that is sometimes greyish or slightly pinky red.

Characteristics
Although of medium weight, ash is a surprisingly strong, tough, elastic timber, with excellent shock-resistance. The grain pattern is similar to oak, but without oak's silver grain. Ash stains and polishes to a handsome finish. It has excellent bending qualities, providing the wood is knot-free.

Uses
Tool handles, sports equipment (including billiard cues) and agricultural implements. Historically, used for making carts, shafts and wheels.

GOLDEN OAK

LIGHT OAK

YELLOW

YEW

TEAK

DARK MAHOGANY

JACOBEAN OAK

ROSEWOOD

BLUE-BLACK

BLUE STAIN

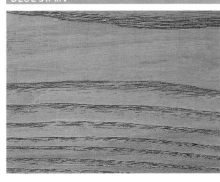

BLEACH

GREEN STAIN

BURNED & WIREBRUSHED

RED STAIN

SINGED

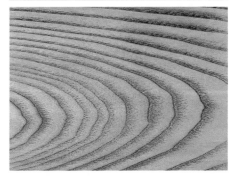

▶ **Take the recommended safety precautions when using a blowtorch.**

BURNING, WIREBRUSHING & LIME

1 Burn the surface with a blowtorch until the wood blackens. Leave to cool.

2 Wirebrush with the grain, then wipe down with a damp cloth to remove char dust.

3 Apply one coat of seal, then sand down.

4 Use a clean cloth to apply lime paste, taking care to cover the surface. Wipe off any surplus.

5 Rub into the grain, using circular motions, then polish to a shine.

6 Final finish.

RHUBARB LEAVES

◀ **Rhubarb leaves are toxic, therefore wash and dry the blender thoroughly after use.**

1 Process rhubarb leaves in a food blender, reducing them to a pulp.

2 Lay the pulp thickly on the surface and leave for 24 hours.

3 Wash off with copious amounts of water. Leave the piece to dry, then sand down.

4 Final finish.

▶ **Liming can be used on any raised-grained wood.**

WIREBRUSHING & WHITE LIME

1 Wirebrush with the grain, then sand lightly.

2 Use a clean lint-free cloth to apply lime paste, taking care to cover the surface. Wipe off any surplus.

3 Rub into the grain, using circular motions. Use a clean cloth to polish to a shine.

4 Final finish.

51

NATURAL

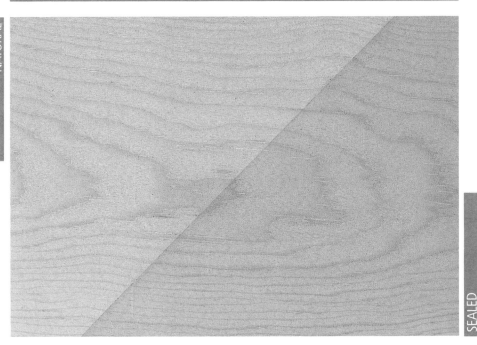

SEALED

Botanical name
Pinus ponderosa.
Also known as
Bird's-eye Pine, Knotty Pine; Western Yellow Pine, Californian White Pine (USA); British Columbian Pine (Canada).
Where grown
Canada and USA.
Colour
Very pale stone, with strong, yellower grain. The heartwood has a reddish tone.

Characteristics
A typical pine, fairly light and soft. It is often very knotty and resinous. The samples shown here are sapwood; the heartwood is much darker. To make working easier (the resin can cause problems), clean the surface with turpentine. Ponderosa Pine is not very durable and has poor steam-bending qualities, but it is extremely stable and takes stain well.

Uses
Furniture, kitchen fittings, window frames, building construction, pattern making. Recently found in ancient American Indian buildings, used as joists.

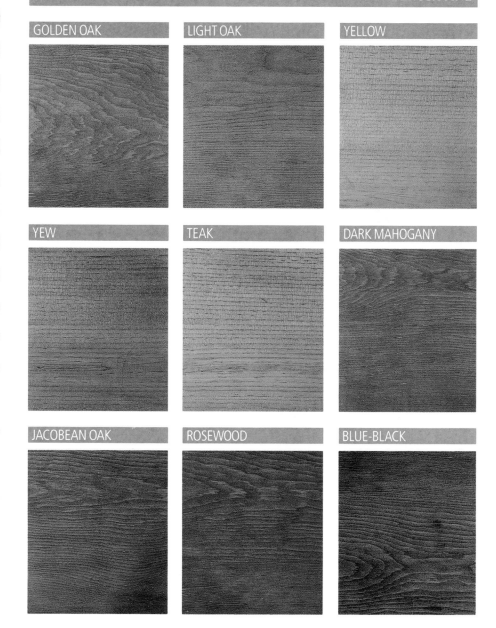

GOLDEN OAK

LIGHT OAK

YELLOW

YEW

TEAK

DARK MAHOGANY

JACOBEAN OAK

ROSEWOOD

BLUE-BLACK

BLUE STAIN

BLEACH

GREEN STAIN

BURNED & WIREBRUSHED

RED STAIN

SINGED

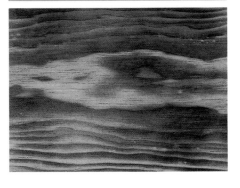

▼ **Ponderosa pine is a softwood and therefore responds well to eroding treatments such as wirebrushing, burning, or even sandblasting.**

1 Wirebrush the prepared surface in the direction of the grain, then lightly sand down the surface with fine abrasive paper.

2 Use a clean lint-free cloth to apply rosewood stain. Work in the direction of the grain. Leave to dry, then lightly sand down.

3 Apply white lime paste with a cloth, wiping off the surplus. Rub into the grain, using circular motions. Use a clean cloth to burnish to a shine.

4 Final finish.

ROSEWOOD STAIN & WHITE LIME

GRAPHITE POWDER

▲**1** Dip a clean lint-free cloth into powdered graphite and rub in with the grain.

2 Use a clean cloth to burnish the surface.

3 Final finish.

► **Ponderosa Pine reacts quite differently to zinc chloride, compared with the way other timbers react.**

1 Pour on enough zinc chloride to cover the surface, and dab it around with a clean lint-free cloth. Leave for 24 hours.

2 Wash off with copious amounts of water. Leave to dry, then sand down.

3 Final finish.

ZINC CHLORIDE

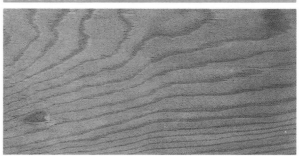

NATURAL

SEALED

Botanical name
Pinus strobus.
Also known as
Yellow Pine (Canada, USA); Eastern White Pine, Northern White Pine, Northern Pine (USA); Quebec Pine, Soft Pine, Weymouth Pine (UK).
Where grown
Canada and USA.
Colour
Pale yellow, with yellow to brown grain.

Characteristics
The heartwood is soft but has an even texture and a very straight grain. White Pine is exceptionally easy to work and takes finishes extremely well, but is not a good timber for steam bending. It is subject to very little movement in use.

Uses
Guitars and organ pipes (because of its resonance), furniture, joinery, construction work. It is an excellent timber for pattern making, carving and turning.

GOLDEN OAK

LIGHT OAK

YELLOW

YEW

TEAK

DARK MAHOGANY

JACOBEAN OAK

ROSEWOOD

BLUE-BLACK

BLUE STAIN

BLEACH

GREEN STAIN

BURNED & WIREBRUSHED

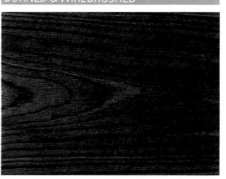

RED STAIN

SINGED

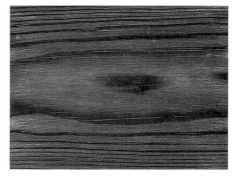

▶ **Heavy wirebrushing gives a characteristic aged finish to softwoods.**

WIREBRUSHING, LIME & ULTRAMARINE PIGMENT

1 Wirebrush the prepared surface in the direction of the grain, then lightly sand down the surface with fine abrasive paper.

2 Mix lime paste with artists' powder pigment, in a ratio of 30:1. Stir the paste until the colour is evenly distributed.

3 Apply with a cloth, wiping off the surplus. Rub into the grain, using circular motions. Use a clean cloth to burnish to a shine.

4 Final finish.

BURNING & LIMING

FABRIC DYE

▲**1** Use a blowtorch to blacken the surface. Leave until the timber has cooled.

2 Wirebrush, following the grain, to remove charred wood; then wipe down with a damp cloth.

3 Seal with shellac sanding sealer, then sand lightly.

4 Use a clean lint-free cloth to apply lime paste, taking care to cover the surface. Wipe off any surplus.

5 Rub into the grain, using circular motions. Use a clean cloth to burnish to a shine.

6 Final finish.

▲**1** Apply undiluted liquid fabric dye, using a clean lint-free cloth. Stain the piece thoroughly, then wipe off any surplus.

2 Rub into the grain, using circular motions. Leave to dry then sand down. Apply more coats, depending on the depth of the colour required.

3 Final finish.

NATURAL

SEALED

Botanical name
Cedrus libani.
Also known as
True Cedar.
Where grown
Middle East.
Colour
Pinkish cream to soft yellow, with occasional brown resin pockets.

Characteristics
A soft, light, brittle timber, with extremely straight close grain. It is very easy to work, and can be eroded easily to create interesting "aged" effects. It stains and finishes well, providing knotty wood is avoided. Although it is durable, it can be susceptible to insect attack. It is said that King Solomon built his temple from Cedar of Lebanon.

Uses
Garden furniture, construction work (in the Middle East), racing boats, interior joinery. Used for lining drawers and cigar boxes, because of its aromatic qualities.

GOLDEN OAK

LIGHT OAK

YELLOW

YEW

TEAK

DARK MAHOGANY

JACOBEAN OAK

ROSEWOOD

BLUE-BLACK

BLUE STAIN

BLEACH

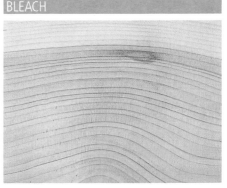

GREEN STAIN

BURNED & WIREBRUSHED

RED STAIN

SINGED

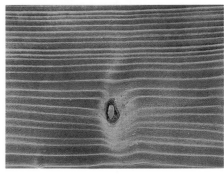

▶ The author used an aluminium cake decoration to brand the timber sample, but any piece of metal can be used. Softwoods respond better to branding than hardwoods. Take great care when carrying out this technique.

BRANDING

1 Use a blowtorch to heat a metal brand; it does not have to be red-hot.

2 Place the brand flat on the surface until the wood just starts to darken. The pattern is used once here, but can be repeated if wished.

3 Final finish.

ZINC CHLORIDE

THINNED EMULSION

▲**1** Pour on enough zinc chloride to cover the surface, and dab it around with a clean lint-free cloth. Leave for 24 hours.

2 Wash off with copious amounts of water. Leave to dry, then sand down.

3 Final finish.

▲**1** Thin emulsion paint with water, in a ratio of 50:50.

2 Use a clean lint-free cloth to apply the paint, then wipe off any surplus.

3 Rub the paint into the grain, using circular motions. Leave to dry.

4 Final finish.

ACKNOWLEDGEMENTS

The author is very grateful for the enthusiastic help he has received from people in the timber trade and expresses his thanks particularly to:

Michael Buckley, American Hardwoods Export Council (Great Britain).
Trans-Atlantic Hardwoods, Colchester, England.
F.T. Morrells & Co. Wood Finishes, Acton, London.
Midland Hardwoods, Bilston, England.
Jo Harding, Research.

Quarto and the publisher would like to thank the following artists and craftsmen for allowing us to reproduce pictures of their work:
Nigel Lofthouse, Nicholas Pryke, John Makepeace.

We are also grateful to the following manufacturers who kindly lent tools and materials for photography:
Rustins Ltd
John Mylands Ltd

Senior Editor Kate Kirby
Senior Art Editor Amanda Bakhtiar
Designer Penny Dawes
Photographers Martin Norris, Paul Forrester
Picture Researcher Anna Kobryn
Art Director Moira Clinch
Publishing Director Janet Slingsby

Typeset by West End Studios, Eastbourne
Manufactured by Bright Arts, Singapore
Printed by Tien Wah, Singapore